Come into the Silence

"Thomas Merton was above all a man of prayer, a thinker who challenged the certitudes of his time and opened new horizons for souls and for the Church."

Pope Francis

"This book offers the gift of meaningful hinges to your day—those threshold times of morning and evening—blessed with the wise words of Thomas Merton. There is such rich simplicity here and an invitation to rest and listen more closely. Spending thirty days with these prayers most surely will deepen your connection to the divine spark within."

Christine Valters Paintner
Online abbess at Abbey of the Arts
Author of *Illuminating the Way*

"*Come into the Silence* is a great gift to both new Merton readers and devoted fans. Even with the wealth of Merton's writings in print, there are surprisingly few guides to incorporating his writings into one's daily prayer. This devotional's well-chosen selections are an accessible way for readers to bring Merton's monastic and contemplative prayer into our busy lives."

Mark C. Meade
Assistant Director
Thomas Merton Center at Bellarmine University

"This book wonderfully opens the wisdom and inspiration of Thomas Merton for daily prayer. Whether you're new to Merton's writings or a longtime reader, *Come into the Silence* is a welcome resource for all interested in deepening their spiritual life and journey of faith."

Daniel P. Horan, O.F.M.
Duns Scotus Chair of Spirituality
Catholic Theological Union
Author of *The Franciscan Heart of Thomas Merton*

Come into the Silence

Thomas Merton

WITH A GREAT SPIRITUAL TEACHER
30 DAYS

AVE MARIA PRESS AVE Notre Dame, Indiana

Series Editor: John Kirvan

Permissions information and credit lines for all material can be found on page 69.

Founded in 1865, Ave Maria Press is a ministry of the United States Province of Holy Cross.

www.avemariapress.com

Paperback: ISBN-13 978-1-64680-041-4

E-book: ISBN-13 978-1-64680-042-1

Cover image © gettyimages.com.

Cover and text design by Katherine Robinson.

Printed and bound in the United States of America.

CONTENTS

WHO IS
THOMAS MERTON?

Thomas Merton was a mid-twentieth-century spiritual master. A Catholic monk, teacher, mystic, poet, and author, he was probably the most popular monastic writer to come along in 1,500 years. Not since St. Augustine in Roman antiquity, with his *Confessions* and *The City of God*, which are still assigned reading to many university and seminary students today, had there been a monastic writer who would be read by so many people as Thomas Merton was in the generations since his work first started to appear, immediately following the Second World War.

His early life was not one of obvious preparation for the monastery. He was baptized into the Church of England, the religious tradition of his father. His mother was a Quaker, but neither parent lived a religiously active life. Merton's mother died when Merton was only six. And he was an orphan, following his father's death, by the age of sixteen.

He lived quite peripatetically, mostly in Bermuda, France, and England, as a child, following his father around as he tried to make a living as a painter and an artist. He also had grandparents on Long Island, New York, and was often left there for long periods of time. This led him to feel rather rootless as a young person.

After attending preparatory school in England, Merton enrolled at Cambridge University and started to shine as a young scholar and intellectual. But after one year, he was kicked out for moral indiscretions. It was discovered that Merton had had a sexual relationship with a young woman, and that she had become pregnant. Merton's godfather and guardian sent him back to his relatives in America, and Merton enrolled at Columbia University in New York City.

It was during his time at Columbia that Merton began to really hunger for God. There had been earlier moments, such as a summer trip to Rome when he mysteriously felt the desire to read the Bible, but for the most part, Merton's teenage and young adult life was filled with raucous friendships, drinking and parties, and the wit and cynicism of young intellectuals.

At Columbia, however, he was blessed with two professors who had a profound influence on him. Mark Van Doren taught him poetry and Daniel Walsh, philosophy. Both men answered the many questions of a searching young man in pursuit of the meaning of life. After Merton's death, Van Doren wrote an obituary of his former student, saying, "I for one have never known a mind more brilliant, more beautiful, more serious, more playful. The energy behind it was immeasurable, and the capacity for love."[1]

Merton soon converted to Roman Catholicism and, in November 1938, was baptized at Corpus Christi Catholic Church, at 121st and Broadway, near the Columbia campus. As he wrote in his autobiography about that day and that momentous time in his life: "What mountains were falling from my shoulders! What scales of dark night were peeling off my intellect, to let in the inward vision of God and His truth!"[2]

Briefly afterward, Merton considered a vocation with the Franciscans. He earned a master's degree in English at Columbia, writing a thesis on the poetry and mysticism of William Blake. He also tried teaching English to college students; he kept trying to write novels; and he worked among the poor, for a short time, in Harlem. In early 1941 he spent a spring break on retreat at the Abbey of Gethsemani, a little-known, severely ascetic monastery in Kentucky. That December, surprising many people who knew him only superficially, Merton gave away most of his possessions and packed the rest in a trunk, heading back to the abbey, hoping never to leave the place again.

He entered Gethsemani as a retreatant hoping to become a novice the very week that the United States declared war on Japan and Germany. Within days, he became Brother Louis, and after many years, he became Father Louis, a priest in addition to a monk. He remained a monk of that monastery for twenty-seven years, until he died an accidental death in Thailand while attending a religious conference of monks gathered from East and West.

When Merton had been publishing poems, trying to write novels, and teaching English at a Franciscan college in New York, he often reflected on how dissatisfied and unhappy he was doing those things. When he entered the monastery, he said that he was happy to give up everything when the large iron gate of the monastery closed behind him. But his abbot (abbots are "spiritual fathers" to their monks) asked the young monk to keep writing. He told Merton that writing could be a form of prayer, and that writing could combine with an ascetical life of service to God. So, Merton kept writing.

Merton wrote many books, one of the first being an autobiography called *The Seven Storey Mountain*, which outsold every other nonfiction book published in 1948 and 1949. The enormous success of *The Seven Storey Mountain* (the author was featured three times in *Time* magazine within one year) also drew hundreds of new vocations—young men—to the monastery in Kentucky. The Second World War had just ended, and people everywhere were seeking answers to questions about life's meaning.

The quiet monastery to which young Merton had retreated had already begun to take on different meaning for him and in his life. He yearned for greater quiet and solitude and wrote about it in another early and personal work, *The Sign of Jonas*, a journal of his early years in the monastery, including the period of time when he was writing *The Seven Storey Mountain* and the months of its early, popular reception. Then there were dozens of other books as well. One of these was *New Seeds of Contemplation*, another bestseller, which has been rightly called one of the most important spirituality books of the twentieth century.

Over the decades, given his bestselling books, his remarkable intellect, vast curiosity, and winsome and outgoing personality, Merton would count among his friends and correspondents other famous writers from around the world—for instance, the poets Boris Pasternak of Russia and Czeslaw Milosz of Poland, who had recently relocated in exile to Northern California. Merton also became a pioneer in interfaith conversations, and came to know now-famous representatives of other religious traditions, including Thich Nhat Hanh, the Vietnamese Buddhist monk; a young Rabbi Zalman Shalomi (later Schachter-Shalomi), the founder of Jewish Renewal, as well as another legendary rabbi, Abraham Joshua Heschel; and H. H. the Dalai Lama, whom Merton visited in Dharamshala, India, in the weeks before Merton died in 1968. Hanh, Shalomi, and Heschel were all able to visit Merton in Kentucky.

Merton's message was deeply Christian and was also informed by all of these complex relationships. He was known for his thoughtful engagement with his own scripture and tradition and for an equally enthusiastic engagement in dialogue and friendship with people of other faiths or no faith. When Pope Francis commended Thomas Merton in a speech before a joint session of the United States Congress, he said, "Merton was above all a man of prayer, a thinker who challenged the certitudes of his time and opened new horizons for souls and for the Church. He was also a man of dialogue, a promoter of peace between peoples and religions."[3]

Although he lived behind monastery walls, during the 1960s Merton became a mentor and friend to many leaders of the antiwar movement in the US and abroad, and he often counseled in person, from Kentucky, or through a vast correspondence with people such as Daniel Berrigan, S.J.; Ernesto Cardenal; and Dorothy Day. He came to realize, soon after his monastic life began, that he could not simply be silent, as in alone with God, to benefit only himself—but that his vocation to a contemplative life must include support, prayer, guidance, and real participation in the struggle of people to find freedom from what binds them.

By the time of his death, Merton enjoyed an international reputation and a slightly uncomfortable fame. As he was by then a cloistered monk, living as a hermit on the monastery property (an eventual, satisfying result of that yearning for more solitude), it was common in the last several years of Merton's life for pilgrims and readers to seek him out, uninvited, wandering up the hill to where his hermitage sat quietly in the woods.

This present work—*Come into the Silence*—is a gathering of essential strands of Merton's spiritual practice and thinking on the subjects of silence, solitude, becoming oneself in Christ, and finding one's true identity not in the world but in service to God. This is presented in a thirty-day format for all who desire to discover some of what he found on his long, personal, and beautifully expressed spiritual journey.

One note about style: Occasionally, male-exclusive language for human beings ("man" and "men") has been silently changed to more inclusive alternatives, without altering any sense or meaning. Such language was common in Merton's early writing, and less so in his later books. We believe he would approve of the emendation.

HOW TO PRAY

THIS BOOK

The purpose of this book is to open a gate for you, to make accessible the spiritual experience and wisdom of one of the most important spiritual teachers of the last seventy-five years.

This is not a book for mere reading. It invites you to meditate and pray its words on a daily basis over a period of thirty days.

Over the course of these thirty days you will engage with topics essential to Merton, which move you toward the theme of silence and deepest communion with God. First, you will work on being real with God and becoming your true self in Christ with his help. Second, you'll begin to love more deliberately and listen more carefully. Third, you'll find quiet inside you and around you. And last, you will settle into the joy of becoming a new person.

This is a handbook for a spiritual journey.

Before you read the "rules" for taking this spiritual journey, remember that this book is meant to free your spirit, not confine it. If on any day the meditation does not resonate well for you, turn elsewhere to find a passage that seems to best fit the spirit of your day and your soul. Don't hesitate to repeat a day as often as you like until you feel that you have discovered what the Spirit, through the words of the author, has to say to your spirit.

Here are suggestions on one way to use this book as a cornerstone of your prayers.

AS YOUR DAY BEGINS

As the day begins, set aside a quiet moment in a quiet place to read the meditation suggested for the day.

The passage is short. It never runs more than a couple hundred words, but it has been carefully selected to give a spiritual focus, a spiritual center to your whole day. It is designed to remind you as another day begins of your own experience at a spiritual level. It is meant to put you in the presence of a spiritual master who is your companion and teacher on this journey. But most of all the purpose of the passage is to remind you that at this moment and at every moment during the day you will be living and acting in the presence of a God who invites you continually but quietly to live in and through him.

A word of advice: Read slowly. Very slowly. The meditation has been broken down into sense lines to help you do just this. Don't read just to get to the end but to savor each part of the meditation. You never know what short phrase, what word, will trigger a response in your spirit. Give the words a chance. After all, you are not just reading this passage; you are praying it. You are establishing a mood of serenity for your whole day. What's the rush?

ALL THROUGH YOUR DAY

Immediately following the day's reading, you will find a sentence or two that we might call a mantra.

This short message is meant as a companion for your spirit as it moves through a busy day. Write it down on a 3" x 5" card or on the appropriate page of your journal. Look at it as often as you can. Repeat it quietly to yourself, and go on your way.

It is meant not to stop you in your tracks or to distract you from your responsibilities but simply, gently, to remind you of the presence of God and your desire to respond to this presence.

AS YOUR DAY IS ENDING

This is the time for letting go of the day.

Find a quiet place and quiet your spirit. Breathe deeply. Inhale, exhale—slowly and deliberately, again and again until you feel your body let go of its tension.

Now read the morning prayer slowly, phrase by phrase. You may recognize at once that we have taken one of the most familiar prayers of the Christian tradition and woven into it phrases taken from the meditation with which you began your day and the mantra that has accompanied you all through your day. In this way a simple evening prayer gathers together the spiritual character of the day that is now ending as it began—in the presence of God.

It is a time for summary and closure.

Invite God to embrace you with love and to protect you through the night.

Sleep well.

SOME OTHER WAYS TO USE THIS BOOK

1. Use it any way your spirit suggests. As mentioned earlier, skip a passage that doesn't resonate for you on a given day, or repeat for a second day or even several days a passage whose richness speaks to you. The truths of the spiritual life are not absorbed in a day, or for that matter, in a lifetime. So take your time. Be patient with the Lord. Be patient with yourself.

2. Take two passages or their mantras and "bang" them together. Spend some time discovering how their similarities or differences illumine your path.

3. Start a spiritual journal to record or deepen your experience of this thirty-day journey. Using either the mantra or another phrase from the reading that appeals to you, write a spiritual account of your day, a spiritual reflection. Create your own meditation.

4. Join millions who are seeking to deepen their spiritual life by forming a small group. More and more people are doing just this to support each other in their mutual quest. Meet once a week, or at least every other week, to discuss and pray about one of the meditations. There are many books and guides available to help you make such a group effective.

John Kirvan, Series Editor

THIRTY DAYS WITH

THOMAS MERTON

DAY ONE

···

My Day Begins

All people seek peace first of all with
themselves.
That is necessary because we do not naturally
find rest even in our own being. We have to
learn to commune with ourselves
before we can communicate with other people
and with God.
A person who is not at peace with himself . . .
projects his interior fighting into the society of
those he lives with
and spreads a contagion of conflict all around
him. . . .
We must withdraw ourselves . . . from effects
that are beyond our control
and be content with the good will and the
work that are the quiet expression of our inner
life.
We must be content to live without watching
ourselves live,
to work without expecting an immediate
reward,

to love without an instantaneous satisfaction,
and to exist without any special recognition.
(*No Man Is an Island*, pp. 120–21)

ALL THROUGH THE DAY

I need rest and peace today. Help me to settle
down, to find peace inside, to find you.

MY DAY IS ENDING

This day is coming to a close, and I am not
sure I'm any better off now
than I was when it began, but I am trying.
I am working to discover what troubles me
and prevents me from being in silence with
God.
I'm working on not just watching myself live.
I am looking for Your wisdom to quiet the
noise inside me,
and to focus my attention on what matters
most.
I am told that this is the work of a lifetime,
but I hope it is much quicker than that.

DAY TWO

My Day Begins

We are warmed by fire, not by the smoke of
the fire.
We are carried over the sea by a ship, not by
the wake of a ship.
So too, what we are is to be sought in the
invisible depths of our own being,
not in our outward reflection in our own acts.
We must find our real selves not in the froth
stirred up by the impact
of our being upon the beings around us, but in
our own soul. . . .
Why do we have to spend our lives
striving to be something
that we would never want to be, if we only
knew what we wanted?
Why do we waste our time doing things which,
if we only stopped to think about them,
are just the opposite of what we were made
for?
We cannot be ourselves unless we know
ourselves.
(*No Man Is an Island*, pp. 117, 126)

ALL THROUGH THE DAY

I spend too much time watching myself living;
today, I'll live in Your present moment.

MY DAY IS ENDING

If I take a moment to list what is beyond my
control,
it can make me feel dizzy or sick.
There's what happens at work.
There's what happens at home.
And then there is the safety of my loved ones.
And future hopes and dreams, for me and
others.
Even my own health. Uncertainty surrounds
me;
what I'm not in control of dwarfs what is
clearly just mine to handle.
I usually don't know what to do with the
worries in my life.
They *are* worries—there is no use lying to
You.
So there it is, and there they are.

DAY THREE

....

I know I will possess all things if I am empty
of all things,
and only You can at once empty me of all
things and fill me with Yourself. . . .
This will be my solitude, to be separated from
myself
so far as to be able to love You alone. . . .
I no longer desire to be myself, but to find
myself transformed in You,
so that there is no more "myself" but only
Yourself.
And that is when I will be what You have
willed to make me from all eternity:
not myself, but Love. And thus will be fulfilled
in me,
as You will it to be fulfilled, Your reason for
the creation of the world and of me in it.

(*Entering the Silence*, p. 49)

ALL THROUGH THE DAY

Help me find some of Your true solitude
today, which I know can be present even
when I am busy and with other people.

MY DAY IS ENDING

What would a transformation of me look like?
What would happen in me, and through me,
if there were far less of me and much more of
You?
What would happen if I felt secure reaching
for the unknown?
I'm not yet sure of the answers to any of these
questions,
and honestly, the questions themselves leave
me feeling anxious.
But this is the process of conversion,
and I want to discover who I am
meant to become, and I know that that will
happen only through You.

DAY FOUR

....

My Day Begins

There is no greater disaster in the spiritual life
than to be immersed
in unreality. . . . When our life feeds on
unreality, it must starve.
It must therefore die. The death by which we
enter into life is not an
escape from reality but a complete gift of
ourselves which involves a total
commitment to reality. It begins by
renouncing the illusory reality which
created things acquire when they are seen
only in their relation to
our own selfish interests. . . . We cannot see
things in perspective
until we cease to hug them to our own bosom.
When we let go of them we begin to
appreciate them as they really are.
Only then can we begin to see God in them.
(*Thoughts in Solitude*, pp. 3–4)

ALL THROUGH THE DAY

I want to find my real self, and I know I can
only find it in only You.

MY DAY IS ENDING

With this inner self we have to come to terms
in silence.
That is the reason for choosing silence.
In silence we have to admit the gap
between the depths of our being, which we
consistently ignore,
and the surface which is untrue to our own
reality.
We recognize the need to be at home with
ourselves in order that we may go out to meet
others,
not just with a mask of affability,
but with real commitment and authentic love.
(*Love and Living*, p. 37)

DAY FIVE

··

My Day Begins

My Lord God, I have no idea where I am
going.
I do not see the road ahead of me.
I cannot know for certain where it will end.
Nor do I really know myself, and the fact that
I think that I am
following your will does not mean that I am
actually doing so.
But I believe that the desire to please you does
in fact please you.
And I hope I have that desire in all that I am
doing.
I hope that I will never do anything apart from
that desire.
And I know that if I do this you will lead me
by the right road though
I may know nothing about it. Therefore, will I
trust you always though
I may seem to be lost and in the shadow of
death.

I will not fear, for you are ever with me, and
you will never leave me
to face my perils alone.
(*Thoughts in Solitude*, p. 79)

ALL THROUGH THE DAY

I will focus on my desires today. Who I am is
what I desire.

MY DAY IS ENDING

We live in a time of great uncertainty. In fact,
has there ever been a time of certainty in my
life?
I don't think there ever has.
But I know that I'm no different from anyone
else,
that there is never certainty in the things of
this world,
and that there is a sure footing in only faith
and hope and the love of God.
I don't face these uncertainties alone. I know.
I may not be able to see where I am going,
but that doesn't mean I cannot see You,
and follow You.

DAY SIX

··

My Day Begins

The desert was the region in which the
Chosen People had
wandered for forty years, cared for by God
alone.
They could have reached the Promised Land
in a few months if they had travelled directly
to it.
God's plan was that they should learn to love
Him and that they should
always look back upon the time in the desert
as the idyllic time of
their life with Him alone.
The desert was simply created to be itself,
not to be transformed by us into something
else. . . .
The desert is . . . the logical dwelling place for
the one who seeks to
be nothing but oneself—that is to say,
a creature solitary and poor and dependent
upon no one but God.
(*Thoughts in Solitude*, p. 5)

ALL THROUGH THE DAY

What is my desert? I know my desert is good
for me, but I need to see how.

MY DAY IS ENDING

I know I need to trust God and not allow my
deserts to make me
so afraid and to worry me so much.
I know I need to be willing to wander
and to look and listen. I need to allow You
to lead me in the wandering and looking and
listening.
Of course, I'm not supposed to know all of
the answers, or even where I'm going.
I don't know the answers!
And I don't know where I am going!
I know that's what faith is about.
Doesn't mean I like it all the time.
Give me more faith, God.
And remind me: Is my desire for faith in itself
a kind of faith?
I hope so. Amen.

DAY SEVEN

My Day Begins

I use up my life in the desire for pleasures and
the thirst for experiences,
for power, honor, knowledge and love, to
clothe this false self
and construct its nothingness into something
objectively real.
And I wind experiences around myself and
cover myself
with pleasures and glory like bandages in
order to make myself
perceptible to myself and to the world, as if I
were an invisible body
that could only become visible when
something visible
covered its surface.
But there is no substance under the things
with which I am clothed.
I am hollow, and my structure of pleasures
and ambitions
has no foundation. I am objectified in them.
But they are all destined by their very
contingency to be destroyed.

And when they are gone there will be nothing
left of me but
my own nakedness and emptiness and
hollowness,
to tell me that I am my own mistake.
(*New Seeds of Contemplation*, p. 35)

All Through the Day

I don't want to live this false self anymore.

My Day Is Ending

Dear God,
This person I've been so busy being, for so
long, pretending to be what I'm not,
worried about recognition, has been like
wearing a lot of masks.
Some of those masks were put on me by
others.
Some of them were completely my own doing.
I'm exhausted trying to be that person who
I'm not.
I'm discovering anew who I am in You,
and I feel that I'm coming into my own, as
I simultaneously come more and more into
Your presence.
I praise and thank you for this.

DAY EIGHT

∙∙

My Day Begins

Oh my God, I don't care about anything;
all I know is that I want to love You.
I want my will to disappear in Your will.
I want to be one spirit with You.
I want to become all Your desires and
thoughts.
I want to live in the middle of Your Trinity
and praise You
with the flames of Your own praise.
Oh my God, knowing all this, why do You
leave me alone
in my selfishness and in my vanity and pride
instead of drawing me into the midst of Your
love? My God, do not delay any longer to
make me a saint and to make me One with
You, and do not delay to live in me.
And if it requires sacrifice, You will give me
the courage to make all sacrifices.
And You will consume me in Your own
immense love.

So do not be afraid of my weakness, oh God,
because You can do everything. I believe in
Your love above all things.
I have forgotten everything else (that is, I
want to).
I live for Your love if You will only make me
live so.
(*Entering the Silence*, pp. 67–68)

ALL THROUGH THE DAY

Show me your love today and this week. Fill
me with Your love, and show me where to
show that love to others.

MY DAY IS ENDING

I have only time for eternity, which is to say
for love, love, love. . . .
Love is pushing me around the monastery,
love is kicking me all around
like a gong I tell you, love is the only thing
that makes it possible
for me to continue to tick. . . . To be led and
moved by the

love of God: indifferent to everything except
that.

This is the source of the only true joy.

(*The Sign of Jonas*, pp. 120, 172)

DAY NINE

MY DAY BEGINS

It is the Holy Ghost that will transform me,
sanctify me. . . .
My own natural powers are helpless. I can do
nothing about it. . . .
If I wait upon the Holy Ghost with desire, this
great gift Who is God will
be given to me. And it is like a kind of an
awakening,
a sort of intimation of all that may happen the
day after tomorrow—
what tremendous possibilities! . . .
Meanwhile I will do everything I can to
remain empty.
My only desire is to give myself completely to
the action of this infinite love
Who is God, Who demands to transform me
into Himself secretly, darkly,
in simplicity, in a way that has no drama
about it and is infinitely
beyond everything spectacular and
astonishing,
so is its significance and its power. . . .
We have got to let God do His will in us.

His Spirit must work in us and not our own.
But since original sin, we always tend to work
against Him when we
work under our own direction.
(*Entering the Silence*, pp. 48, 52)

All Through the Day

Wake me all day today to Your presence.
Make Your Holy Spirit present in me in such
a way that Your love is obvious to everyone I
come into contact with.

My Day Is Ending

I want the Holy Spirit to fill me.
Unholy things in the world should leave me.
God wants my whole life, my full life, and the
things around me
sometimes just get in the way.
I often wonder what I might do if I ever let the
Holy Spirit
really transform me the way that I know can
happen.
I've had glimpses of the Holy Spirit's power in
my life in the past.
I want those glimpses to become more like
sustaining breath now.

DAY TEN

....

MY DAY BEGINS

If I were to make any resolutions, it would be
the same old ones—
no need to make them—they have been made.
No need to reflect on them—it doesn't take
much concentration
to see how I keep them. I struggle along.
It is useless to break your head over the same
old details week after week
and year after year, pruning the same ten
twigs off the top of the tree.
Get at the *root*: union with God.
On these days drop everything and hide in
yourself to find Him in the silence
where He is hidden with you, and listen to
what He has to say. . . .
There is only one thing to live for: love.
There is only one unhappiness: not to love
God.
That is what pains me . . . to see my own soul
so full of movement
and shadows and vanities, cross-currents of

dry wind,
stirring up the dust and rubbish of desire.
(*Entering the Silence*, p. 64)

All Through the Day

I know what needs to be done in my life. Give
me the patience and forbearance to actually
do it!

My Day Is Ending

God's silence is God's gift to me and to any
who truly desire it.
I am finding You, God, in that silence, where
it turns out that
You were there all along.
I hear You speaking to me in that silence,
and then I realize that You were there, waiting
for me, to be heard.
Why has this taken me so long to discover?
And have I truly discovered it?
What more is there for me to find?
I know the answer, at least in part:
because I don't actually discover or find the
answer;
I am simply remembering it again.

DAY ELEVEN

··

My Day Begins

Love sails me around the house.
I walk two steps on the ground and four steps
in the air.
It is love. It is consolation. I don't care if it is
consolation.
I am not attached to consolation. I love God.
Love carries me all around. I don't want to do
anything but love.
And when the bell rings [telling the monks it
is time for prayer in choir]
it is like pulling teeth to make myself shift
because of that love,
secret love, hidden love, obscure love, down
inside me and outside me
where I don't care to talk about it. . . .
You have got to be all the time cooperating
with love . . . and love
sets a fast pace even at the beginning and if
you don't keep up you'll
get dropped. And yet any speed is too slow for
love—and no

speed is too fast for you if you will only let
love drag you off your feet—
after that you will have to sail the whole way.
(*The Sign of Jonas*, pp. 120–21)

All Through the Day

I will go that inner place today whenever I
begin to forget Your precious love.

My Day Is Ending

What can I do when the love of God that I
know is very real
is not very real or even obvious to me?
Even the most extraordinary people—saints
like Mother Teresa—
have gone days, even years, without feeling
the love of God that they
still somewhere knew was there.
Is it possible that this secret, hidden love
can sometimes remain secret and hidden even
to the one
who possesses it? And if it does,
what do I do with my feelings of loneliness
and feeling unloved?
This must be a time for faith and hope, and
this must be why the Apostle

said that "faith, hope, and love abide, these
three" (1 Cor 13:13).
There are times when they are not equally
experienced in life,
but they all remain, and remain together.

DAY TWELVE

My Day Begins

There is nothing else worth living for: only
this infinitely peaceful love,
Who is beyond words, beyond emotion,
beyond intelligence.
Cradle me, Holy Spirit, in your dark silver
cloud and protect me
against the heat of my own speech, my own
judgments, my own vision.
Ward off the sickness of consolation and
desire,
of fear and grief that spring from desire.
I will give You my will for You to cleanse and
rinse of
all this clay.
(*Entering the Silence*, p. 49)

All Through the Day

This is a tough lesson, so I'm sorry that I
keep returning to it, but I also know that You
know how the things of the world can be so
tempting.

My Day Is Ending

What am I really living for?
I have to be honest with myself.
If I can't do that—be honest with myself—then
I haven't made any progress
in the spiritual life at all.
I am living for many, many things, and many
of them have very
little to do with desire for God's will and
presence in my life.
So now, once again—and I'm beginning to see
that this is a daily need—
I am giving this, too, to God, and I'm saying,
very simply,
I want to do better.
When, O God, will I be doing better!?
I want to experience the full and complete
love of God.
God help me.

DAY THIRTEEN

MY DAY BEGINS

It is God's love that warms me in the sun and
God's love
that sends the cold rain. It is God's love that
feeds me in the bread I eat,
and God that feeds me also by hunger and
fasting.
It is the love of God that sends the winter days
when I am cold and sick
and the hot summer when I labor and my
clothes are full of sweat:
but it is God Who breathes on me with light
winds off the river
and in the breezes out of the wood.
His love spreads the shade of the sycamore
over my head. . . .
It is God's love that speaks to me in the birds
and streams;
but also behind the clamor of the city God
speaks to me in His judgments,
and all these things are seeds sent to me from
His will.
If these seeds would take root in my liberty,
and if His will would grow from my freedom,

I would become the love that He is, and my
harvest would be
His glory and my own joy.
(*New Seeds of Contemplation*, pp. 16–17)

ALL THROUGH THE DAY

Your love is what I need.

MY DAY IS ENDING

Dear God,
When Your love surrounds me, I often feel it
like
a warm sun; and when Your love asks me to
sacrifice something
that I have to sacrifice, it can feel much less
comfortable.
At those times, I admit, divine love can feel
like human loss.
But You remind me how all of this—both the
warmth and the sacrifice—
is part of Your love for me.
You are my life and my all.
And I am learning, with Your help, to be
present with
You in every way that Your love comes down.
Give me strength to do that. Amen.

DAY FOURTEEN

My Day Begins

My chief care should not be to find pleasure or
success, health or life
or money or rest or even things like virtue and
wisdom—still less
their opposites: pain, failure, sickness, death.
But in all that happens,
my one desire and my one joy should be to
know:
"Here is the thing that God has willed for me.
In this His love is found,
and in accepting this I can give back His love
to Him and give myself with it to Him.
For in giving myself I shall find Him, and He
is life everlasting."
By consenting to His will with joy and doing it
with gladness I have His love
in my heart, because my will is now the same
as His love, and I am
on the way to becoming what He is, Who is
Love.

(*New Seeds of Contemplation*, pp. 17–18)

ALL THROUGH THE DAY

I see Your love not only in my inner life but
also all around me in the world.

MY DAY IS ENDING

Dear God,
This love of yours is much more, I realize,
than what
You are doing in my life.
It is also more than my acceptance of Your
will for me.
Your love is all around me in the world, too,
and not only in what I see as beautiful and
wondrous:
sunsets, birds singing, and flowers in
springtime.
Your love is here in the pursuit of freedom
and justice.
Your love is in the care of the immigrant
and in solidarity with everyone who is lonely,
sad, or in pain.
My response to Your tremendous love needs
to respond to these situations,
too, if I am to be Your hands and feet in
the world around me.
Keep showing me when, and how, and where
I am Your love.

DAY FIFTEEN

God is said to be "found" by the soul that is
united to Him in a bond
as intimate as marriage. And this bond is a
union of spirits, in faith.
Faith, here, means complete fidelity,
the complete gift and abandonment of oneself.
It means perfect trust in a hidden God.
It implies submission to the gentle but
inscrutable guidance
of His infinitely hidden Spirit.
It demands the renunciation of our own lights
and our own
prudence and our own wisdom and of our
whole "self" in order
to live in and by His Spirit.
"He that is joined to the Lord," says St. Paul, "is
one Spirit" (1 Cor 6:17). . . .
To live in Him is to live by His power, to
reach from end to end
of the universe in the might of His wisdom,
to rule and form all things in and with Him.

(*The Silent Life*, p. 3)

ALL THROUGH THE DAY

I trust You even when I cannot see or sense
Your presence.

MY DAY IS ENDING

Your Spirit is here with me, guiding, moving,
inspiring,
challenging, highlighting, pointing me toward
what
You would have me see and feel and do.
How can I better see and understand all of this
activity?
I am discovering this, now, and dear God,
I am sorry to keep asking for what I already
have, and what You
already so graciously do, but could You please
do all of this more,
and more obviously, in my life than ever
before?
Thank you.

DAY SIXTEEN

My Day Begins

My intention is to give myself entirely and
without compromise to
whatever work God wants to do in my soul,
but that work is
nevertheless in a certain sense already
defined by a contemplative vocation.
By that it seems to me that God has signified
a certain path, a certain goal, and I am to keep
that in view:
that is where obedience must tend according
to God's signified will.
That means total renunciation of the business,
ambitions, honors,
activities of the world—a bare minimum of
concern with
temporal necessities.
(*Entering the Silence*, p. 44)

All Through the Day

Inside, with You, I will be quiet today. When
I'm occupied with other things, I will still be
quietly with You.

MY DAY IS ENDING

Dear God,
You know my desire to be with You always,
and You know how
I am learning how a contemplative approach
to prayer,
with silence, Your silence,
can turn my prayer from something routine
and formulaic
into something I experience deep within my
soul.
You tell me that You are there in my soul,
and that I am finding You there every time I
return.
Give me more silence.
Find me in Your silence, that only You can
give.
"For God alone my soul waits in silence,"
David said in the psalm (Ps 62:1).
What sweetness this is.

DAY SEVENTEEN

....

MY DAY BEGINS

Prayer and love are really learned in the hour
when prayer
becomes impossible and your heart turns to
stone.
If you have never had any distractions, you
don't know how to pray.
For the secret of prayer is a hunger for God
and for the vision of God, a hunger that lies far
deeper than the
level of language and affection. . . .
That is why it is useless to get upset when you
cannot shake off distractions. . . .
If you are wise you will not pay any attention
to these things:
remain in simple attention to God and keep
your will
peacefully directed to Him in simple desire
while the intermittent shadows of this
annoying movie go about
in the remote background.
If you are aware of them at all it is only to
realize that you refuse them.

(*New Seeds of Contemplation*, pp. 221–22)

ALL THROUGH THE DAY

Work and family occupy my thoughts
more than they should. But are they really
"distractions"? Not really. They are my loves.
They were given to me by You—and thank
You for them. Still, I cannot truly be in Your
presence without allowing these "distractions"
to settle around me like puddles and to step
outside them into your warm embrace.

MY DAY IS ENDING

It is the will to pray that is the essence of
prayer, and the desire to find God,
to see Him and to love Him, is the one thing
that matters.
If you have desired to know Him and love
Him, you have already done
what was expected of you, and it is much
better to desire God
without being able to think clearly of Him,
than to have marvelous thoughts
about Him without desiring to enter into
union with His will.
(*New Seeds of Contemplation*, p. 224)

DAY EIGHTEEN

My Day Begins

How can I find One Who is nowhere?
If I find Him, I myself will also be nowhere. . . .
How can I find Him Who is everywhere?
If He is everywhere, He is indeed close to me,
and with me, and in me: perhaps He will turn
out to be,
in some mysterious way, my own self.
To be one with One Whom one cannot see is
to be hidden, to be nowhere,
to be no one: it is to be unknown as He is
unknown,
forgotten as He is forgotten, lost as He is lost
to the world which
nevertheless exists in Him.
Yet to live in Him is to live by His power. . . .
to be the hidden
instrument of His Divine action, the minister
of His redemption,
the channel of His mercy, and the messenger
of His
infinite Love.
(*The Silent Life*, pp. 1, 3)

ALL THROUGH THE DAY

Even in my business and busyness I will
"hide" in Your love and mercy.

MY DAY IS ENDING

Dear God,
As evening comes, I'm pondering what has
happened to me
and through me this day. There is so much
going on.
You know this—how noisy daily ordinary life
is.
You have lived as I have lived.
I pray, now, in the near darkness of evening
and of my
own unknowing, that I had some positive
effect of Your
redemption in the world as a result of all that
I've done.
And I will rest in confidence that You have
been
present with me, in the deepest sort of way,
all the while. Amen.

DAY NINETEEN

....

My Day Begins

My intention is to give myself entirely and
without compromise
to whatever work God wants to do in my soul,
but that work is nevertheless . . . already
defined by
a *contemplative* vocation. By that it seems to
me
that God has signified a certain path, a certain
goal,
and I am to keep that in view. . . .
However, the important thing is to live for
God and not for
contemplation. The reason is obvious: because
a contemplative
is not one who lives for contemplation,
but one who lives for God alone.
And that is one thing I need to get good and
straight.
If I am too concerned with my progress in
sanctity,
in contemplation, then I am very definitely
dividing my love and my

energies between God and something that is
less than Him.

(*Entering the Silence*, p. 44)

ALL THROUGH THE DAY

Lord Jesus Christ, Son of God, have mercy on
me, a sinner.

MY DAY IS ENDING

I'm not special or holy, Lord. *You* are holy.
I am, whatever I am, entirely *in You*.
There is no "me," the more that I am learning
to be present in You.
So what's holy about me? Nothing.
Remind me of this, now as ever.
I don't want to ever be like the sanctimonious
ones whom Jesus
rebuked, saying, "You clean the outside of the
cup and of the plate,
but inside they are full of greed and self-
indulgence. . . .
First clean the inside of the cup, so that the
outside also
may become clean" (Mt 23:25–26).

DAY TWENTY

My Day Begins

To discover the Trinity is to discover a deeper
solitude.
The love of the Three Divine Persons holds
your heart
in its strength and builds about you a wall of
quiet that the noise
of exterior things can only penetrate with
difficulty.
You no longer have to strive to resist the world
or escape it:
material things affect you little. And thus, you
use and possess
them as you should, for you dominate them,
in making them serve the ends
of prayer and charity, instead of letting them
dominate you
with the tyranny of your own selfishness. . . .
Once God has called you to solitude,
everything you touch leads you further into
solitude.
(*The Sign of Jonas*, pp. 74, 333–34)

ALL THROUGH THE DAY

My deeper solitude is my balm and my
teacher.

MY DAY IS ENDING

Dear Father, Son, and Holy Spirit,
You create me,
You reach toward me,
You inspire me to be better.
Lead me now deeper into Your solitude.
Show me into that quiet place where there is
no striving and struggling,
or selfishness and craving, but the simple
satisfaction of knowing
that I am in You, and You are in me. Amen.

DAY TWENTY-ONE

My Day Begins

How simple it is to find God in solitude.
There is no one else, nothing else. He is all
there is to find there.
Everything is in Him. And what could be more
pleasing to Him
than that we should leave all things and all
company to be with Him
and think only of Him and know Him alone,
in order to give Him our love? . . .
If I am called to solitude it is, I think, to
unlearn all tension
and get rid of the strain that has always
falsified me in
the presence of others and put harshness into
the words of my mind.
If I have needed solitude, it is because I have
always so much needed
the mercy of Christ and needed His humility
and His charity.
How can I give love unless I have much more
than I have ever had?

(*A Search for Solitude*, p. 28)

ALL THROUGH THE DAY

I need Your silence, Your mercy, Your love.

MY DAY IS ENDING

I don't want to be spiritual, Lord.
I want You.
I don't want to be humble and pure and holy.
I want You.
In this silence, where I am with You,
and where I am not trying to do anything,
or be anything,
or be anyone to try and impress someone else,
I find I am able to rest and to find the one
thing I need.
I am like that merchant of fine pearls
who then discovers one of incredible value.
"He went and sold all that he had and bought
it" (Mt 13:46).

DAY TWENTY-TWO

MY DAY BEGINS

Union with Christ means unity in Christ, so
that each one who is in Christ
can say, with Paul: "It is now not I that live but
Christ that lives in me."
It is the same Christ who lives in all.
The individual has "died" with Christ to his
"old man," his exterior,
egotistical self, and "risen" in Christ. . . .
In any case, the "death of the old man" is not
the destruction of
personality but the dissipation of an illusion,
and the discovery of the
new man is the realization of what was there
all along,
at least as a radical possibility,
by reason of the fact that man is the image of
God.
(*Zen and the Birds of Appetite*, pp. 117–18)

ALL THROUGH THE DAY

Christ within me means less and less of the
old me.

MY DAY IS ENDING

St. John of the Cross compares us to a window
through which the light of God is shining.
If the windowpane is clean of every stain, it is
completely transparent,
we do not see it at all: it is "empty" and
nothing is seen but the light.
(*Zen and the Birds of Appetite*, p. 119)

Dear God, wipe me clean.
Make me a glass that shines through for you.
Make me empty of all that is vain and
meaningless,
so that what people see, when they look at
me, is You.
I know that the more I disappear, the more
You will appear,
and the more I shine, the less it will be me
who is shining
but rather Your love living and shining in me.
May that happen. Amen.

TWENTY-THREE

My Day Begins

"If I have perfect faith . . . but no Love, I am
nothing" (1 Corinthians 13:2). . . .
In fact, the object of faith is One—God, Love.
And though the revealed doctrines about Him
are true,
yet what they tell us of Him is not fully
adequate as long as
we grasp them only separately, incoherently,
without living unity in Love.
They must converge upon Love as the spokes of
a wheel converge upon a central hub.
They are window frames through which the
One Light enters
our houses. The window frame is precise and
distinct:
yet what we really see is the light itself,
which is diffuse and all-pervading, so that it is
everywhere and nowhere.
(*Love and Living*, p. 18)

ALL THROUGH THE DAY

I have been told, and have learned, many
things about You, but I don't yet know you as
I should.

MY DAY IS ENDING

No mind can comprehend God's reality, as it is
in itself,
and if we approach Him, we must advance not
only by knowing
but by not-knowing.
We must seek to communicate with Him, not
only by words,
but above all by silence, in which there is only
the One Word,
and the One Word is infinite Love
and endless silence. . . . Where is silence?
Where is solitude? Where is Love?
Ultimately, these cannot be found anywhere
except in the ground of
our own being. There is perfect peace,
because we are grounded
in infinite creative and redemptive Love.
(*Love and Living*, p. 18)

TWENTY-FOUR

My Day Begins

Everyone has a vocation to be someone:
but we must understand clearly that in order
to fulfill this vocation
we can only be one person: ourselves. . . .
What does this mean? We must be ourselves
by being Christ. . . .
A person only lives as a person when he
knows truth and loves what
he knows and acts according to what he loves.
In this way
he becomes the truth that he loves.
So we "become" Christ by knowledge and by
love.
(*No Man Is an Island*, pp. 133–34)

All Through the Day

I am finding what it means for me to be Christ
in the world.

My Day Is Ending

To be what we are meant to be, we must know
Christ, and love Him,
and do what He did. Our destiny is in our own
hands since God
has placed it there and given us His grace to
do the impossible.
It remains for us to take up courageously and
without hesitation the work
He has given us, which is the task of living our
own life
as Christ would live it in us. . . . It takes
intrepid courage to live according to
the truth, and there is something of
martyrdom in every truly Christian life. . . .
Our vocation is precisely this: to bear witness
to the truth of Christ
by laying down our lives at His bidding. . . .
This testimony need not take
the special form of a political and public death
in defense
of Christian truth or virtue. But we cannot
avoid the "death" of our own will,
of our own natural tendencies, of the
inordinate passions of our flesh,

and of our whole selfish "being," in order to
submit ourselves to
what our own conscience tells us to be the
truth and
the will of God and the inspiration of the Spirit
of Christ.

(*No Man Is an Island,* pp. 134–35)

TWENTY-FIVE

My Day Begins

Today, in a moment of trial, I rediscovered
Jesus,
or perhaps discovered Him for the first time.
But then, in a monastery you are always
discovering Jesus for the first time.
Anyway, I came closer than ever to fully
realizing how true it is that our relations
with Jesus are something utterly beyond the
level of imagination and emotion.
His eyes, which are the eyes of Truth, are
fixed
upon my heart. Where His glance falls, there
is peace:
for the light of His Face, which is the Truth,
produces truth wherever it shines.
There too is joy. And he says to those he loves,
I will fix my eyes upon you . . . . The grace of
this gaze of Christ
upon my heart transfigured this day like a
miracle.

It seems to me that I have discovered a
freedom that
I never knew before in my life.
(*Entering the Silence*, p. 403)

All Through the Day

The gaze of Christ is upon me.

My Day Is Ending

How do I balance this feeling I have—of
wanting nothing more than
to sit quietly in Your presence, to be seen by
You,
to feel overwhelmed, as I do,
by Your grace and love and attention?
What am I to do with this feeling? I think I will
cherish it.
And when I don't feel it anymore—
because I don't feel it, often,
and it sometimes hurts to remember what it's
like in Your gaze,
just then—I will try to walk still in the
confidence
of Your love for me.
Do you love me equally, all the time,

even when the feeling of Your love has gone
away?
Yes, I will have faith in that truth,
and I will remember the precious other.

TWENTY-SIX

....

My Day Begins

It is all the more necessary, at this time, to
rediscover the climate of
solitude and of silence: not that everyone can
go apart and live alone.
But in moments of silence, of meditation, of
enlightenment and peace,
one learns to be silent and alone everywhere. . . .
One opens the inner door of his heart to the
infinite silences of the Spirit,
out of whose abysses love wells up
without fail and gives itself to all.
In His silence, the meaning of every sound is
finally clear.
Only in His silence can the truth of words be
distinguished, not in their separateness, but in
their pointing to
the central unity of Love.
All words, then, say one thing only: that *all is
Love*.
(*Love and Living*, p. 19)

ALL THROUGH THE DAY

There is a place in me—the most important
part of me—that is silent in You.

MY DAY IS ENDING

If you want to identify me, ask me not where I
live, or what I like to eat,
or how I comb my hair, but ask me what I am
living for, in detail,
ask me what I think is keeping me from living
fully for the thing
I want to live for.

(*My Argument with the Gestapo*, pp. 160–61)

Holy Spirit,
inspire me to be that person who is living fully
for what I truly want to live for. Amen.

TWENTY-SEVEN

My Day Begins

Kanchenjunga[4] this afternoon.
The clouds of the morning parted slightly and
the mountain, the massif of
attendant peaks, put on a great, slow, silent
dorje dance of snow and mist,
light and shadow. . . . Very stately and
beautiful.
Then toward evening the clouds cleared some
more, except for a long apron
of mist and shadow below the main peaks. . . .
Last night I had a curious dream about
Kanchenjunga.
I was looking at the mountain and it was pure
white, absolutely pure,
especially the peaks that lie to the west. And I
saw the pure beauty of their
shape and outline, all in white. And I heard a
voice saying—
or got the clear idea of: "There is another side
to the mountain."
(*The Asian Journal of Thomas Merton*, pp. 155–56, 152)

ALL THROUGH THE DAY

I have the spiritual courage to go into the
unknown.

MY DAY IS ENDING

I am afraid, Holy One, my Lord,
of how exposed I feel when I think
of walking even further into the unknown,
into You.
There is another side to the mountain.
I haven't seen it.
I may never see it, but I desire to reach that
other side.
My help is in You.
You will keep my foot steady.
And in this silence, where You meet me,
I know that You are like
the shade at my right hand (cf. Ps 121:2, 3, 5).

TWENTY-EIGHT

My Day Begins

I wonder if there are twenty people alive in
the world now who
see things as they really are. That would mean
that there
were twenty people who were free, who were
not dominated
or even influenced by any attachment to any
created thing
or to their own selves or to any gift of God,
even to the highest,
the most supernaturally pure of His graces.
I don't believe that there are twenty such
people alive in the world.
But there must be one or two.
They are the ones who are holding everything
together and keeping
the universe from falling apart.
(*New Seeds of Contemplation*, p. 203)

ALL THROUGH THE DAY

Keep me in this place of knowing who I am in
You. I want to be fully alive in Your will and
presence.

MY DAY IS ENDING

My prayer tonight is so simple and yet so very
difficult.
I want to be free from the things that
preoccupy me too much.
I want to love things in the world, without
being preoccupied by them.
I hope to pray with the heart of God, and act
with the hands and feet of God.
I desire to listen to Your voice in my life, and
to follow Your lead.
I know You are there, and I know sometimes
when I am ignoring You.
I am sorry for that.
I am trying each day to give myself more
completely to You.
Help me now and always. Amen.

DAY TWENTY-NINE

MY DAY BEGINS

The ever renewed mission of the Spirit to the
soul that is in the grace of
Christ is . . . the analogy of the natural breath
that keeps renewing,
from a moment to moment, our bodily life.
The mystery of the Spirit is the mystery of
selfless love.
We receive Him in the "inspiration" of secret
love, and we give Him
to others in the outgoing of our own charity.
Our life in Christ is then a life
both of receiving and of giving. We receive
from God, in the Spirit,
and in the same Spirit we return our love to
God through our brothers.
(*New Seeds of Contemplation*, p. 159)

ALL THROUGH THE DAY

Is there evidence of God's love in my life
today?

MY DAY IS ENDING

What does my life in Christ mean, after all?
What is this secret love of God that pours
into my heart, but God's life pouring into me,
for me,
changing me, making me a new creature,
hopefully a more godly creature who is
identified fully and only in and through and
by that secret love?
Am I sending that love out of me, or am I
hoarding it for myself?
It is possible to hoard it, I think.
But a personal and secret love is not meant to
be an exclusive love.
Such a love as this is supposed to move easily
through me, to others.
May it be so in me, today, tonight, and always.
Amen.

DAY THIRTY

∙∙

MY DAY BEGINS

If I have this divine life in me,
what do the accidents of pain and pleasure,
hope and fear, joy and sorrow matter to me?
They are not my life and they have little to do
with it.
Why should I fear anything that cannot rob
me of God,
and why should I desire anything that cannot
give me
possession of Him?
(*New Seeds of Contemplation*, p. 159)

ALL THROUGH THE DAY

I'm here in Your silence. Keep me close, even
and especially now that these thirty days are
coming to an end.

MY DAY IS ENDING

Exterior things come and go, but why should
they disturb me?

Why should joy excite me or sorrow cast me
down,
achievement delight me or failure depress me,
life attract or death repel me
if I live only in the Life that is within me by
God's gift?
Why should I worry about losing a bodily life
that I must inevitably lose
anyway, as long as I possess a spiritual life and
identity that cannot
be lost against my desire?
Why should I fear to cease to be what I am not
when I have already become
something of what I am?
Why should I go to great labor to possess
satisfactions that cannot last an hour,
and which bring misery after them, when I
already own God in His
eternity of joy? It is the easiest thing in the
world to possess this life
and this joy; all you have to do is believe and
love;
and yet people waste their whole lives
in appalling labor and difficulty and sacrifice
to get things
that make real life impossible.

(*New Seeds of Contemplation*, p. 160)

ONE FINAL WORD

This book was created to be nothing more than a gateway—a gateway to the spiritual wisdom of a specific teacher and a gateway opening on your own spiritual way.

You may decide that Thomas Merton is someone whose experience of God is one that you wish to follow more closely and deeply, in which case you should get a copy of one of the books quoted in this text and pray it as you have prayed this gateway journey.

You may decide that his experience has not helped you. There are many other teachers. Somewhere there is the right teacher for your own, very special, absolutely unique journey of the spirit. You will find your teacher. You will discover your path.

We would not be searching, as St. Augustine reminds us, if we had not already been found.

NOTES

1. Mark Van Doren's obituary first appeared January 4, 1969, and was republished by America Media: Mark Van Doren, "Thomas Merton's Obituary from 1969," *America: The Jesuit Review*, December 10, 2018, https://www.americamagazine.org.

2. Thomas Merton, *The Seven Storey Mountain* (New York: Mariner Books, 1999), 244.

3. Excerpts from Pope Francis's speech before the US Congress are available on the website of the Abbey of Gethsemani: "Pope Francis Speaks about Thomas Merton in His Address to Congress," Abbey News, September 24, 2015, http://www.monks.org.

4. Kanchenjunga is the third highest mountain in the world, found in the Himalayas, where Merton visited on pilgrimage in the weeks and months before he died, and where he wrote these words.

PERMISSIONS

All the scripture quotes in the various pieces are left just as they were presented by Merton in his time. His translations were often his own, and they approximate closely to those that appeared in the *New American Bible*. All scripture quotations not in Merton quotations are taken from the *New Revised Standard Version* (NRSV), New Revised Standard Version Bible, copyright 1989, Division of Christian Education of the National Council of the Churches of Christ in the United States of America. Used by permission. All rights reserved.

Ave Maria Press is grateful to the publishers who have allowed excerpts from Merton works to be included in this book. Full credit lines are listed below.

The Asian Journal of Thomas Merton, copyright ©1975 by The Trustees of the Merton Legacy Trust. Reprinted by permission of New Directions Publishing Corp.

THOMAS MERTON (1915–1968) is widely acclaimed as one of the most influential spiritual masters of the twentieth century. A Trappist monk of the Abbey of Gethsemani, Kentucky, he was a poet, social activist, and student of comparative religion. In 1949, he was ordained to the priesthood and given the name Fr. Louis. Merton wrote more than seventy books, mostly on spirituality, social justice, and pacifism, as well as scores of essays and reviews, including his best-selling autobiography, *The Seven Storey Mountain*.

30 DAYS
with a **GREAT** Spiritual Teacher

Each book in the 30 Days with a Great Spiritual Teacher series provides a month of daily readings from one of Christianity's most beloved spiritual guides. For each day there is a brief and accessible morning meditation drawn from the mystic's writings, a simple mantra for use throughout the day, and a night prayer to focus one's thoughts as the day ends. These easy-to-use books are the perfect prayer companion for busy people who want to root their spiritual practice in the solid ground of these great spiritual teachers.

TITLES IN THE SERIES INCLUDE: